Cowgirl

Cowgirl

◆

MERIDETH McGREGOR

Walker and Company   New York

First published in the United States of America in 1992 by Walker Publishing Company, Inc.

Published simultaneously in Canada by Thomas Allen & Son Canada, Limited, Markham, Ontario

Library of Congress Cataloging-in-Publication Data
McGregor, Merideth.
    Cowgirl / Merideth McGregor.
        p.   cm.
    Summary: Casey describes her life on a Texas ranch with her parents, dogs, horses, and cows.
    ISBN 0-8027-8170-5 (cloth). —ISBN 0-8027-8171-3
    1. Farm life—Juvenile literature. 2. Cowgirls—Juvenile literature. [1. Ranch life.] I. Title.
S519.M32   1992
636.2'01'0924—dc20   91-47894
                                                      CIP
                                                      AC

Book Design by Georg Brewer

Printed in the United States of America

10   9   8   7   6   5   4   3   2   1

Hi, y'all! My name is Casey and I'm a cowgirl. I live on the T13 Ranch in Paris, Texas. I live here with my mom and dad, my dogs, Sissy and Lilly and their puppies, our horses, Sally, Grey, and Willie, and 300 cows that don't have names.

My mom grew up here too, and she's teaching me to be a cowgirl just like my grandparents taught her. There are a lot of things to learn.

We work hard every day on the ranch. Mom, Dad, and I start our day at 5:30 A.M. After a big breakfast we get in the pickup and drive to the fields, where we begin our work.

Each season brings new chores. In springtime we plant our crops. We plant soybeans, hay, and maize—a type of corn. With lots of sunshine and rain they grow very tall. The maize grows even taller than me!

In the summer we harvest the fields of hay. We use a machine called a swather to cut the hay.

It takes Mom and me almost all day to cut a whole field. Sometimes I get bored.

After Mom cuts the hay, Dad comes along with a haybaler. The haybaler rolls the hay into a big ball called a bale.

Sometimes, when Mom and Dad are finished, my cousin April and I take a ride through the fields and play with the big bales of hay. They make good hiding places for a game of hide-and-seek.

In the fall we harvest the soybean and maize. We use the maize to feed our cows. My parents sell the soybeans to the feed mill in Roxton, the next town over.

During the winter, when there is no grass for grazing, we load up the truck with bales of hay and drive out to the fields.

The bales are held together by wire. My mom cuts
the wire and we throw the hay to the hungry cows. My
mom is really strong. Someday I'll be as strong as her.

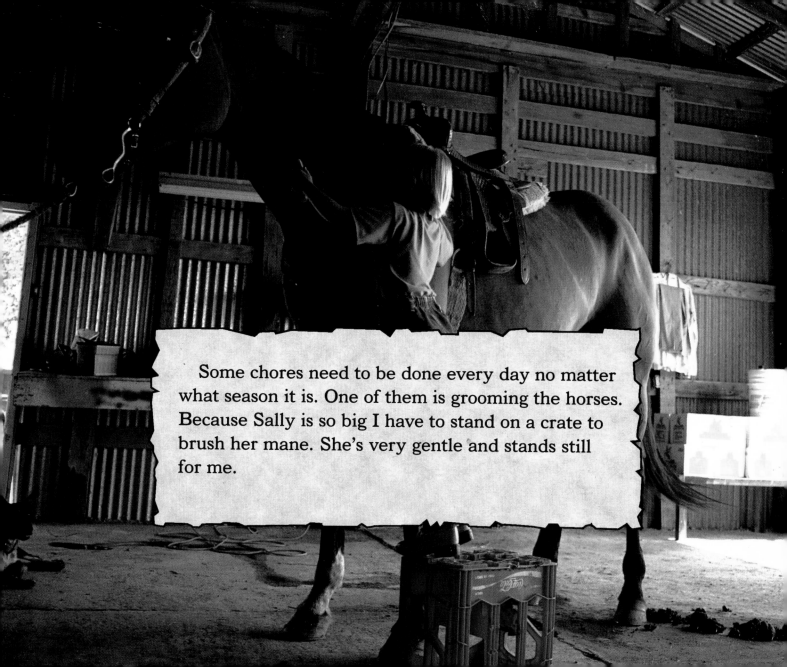

Some chores need to be done every day no matter what season it is. One of them is grooming the horses. Because Sally is so big I have to stand on a crate to brush her mane. She's very gentle and stands still for me.

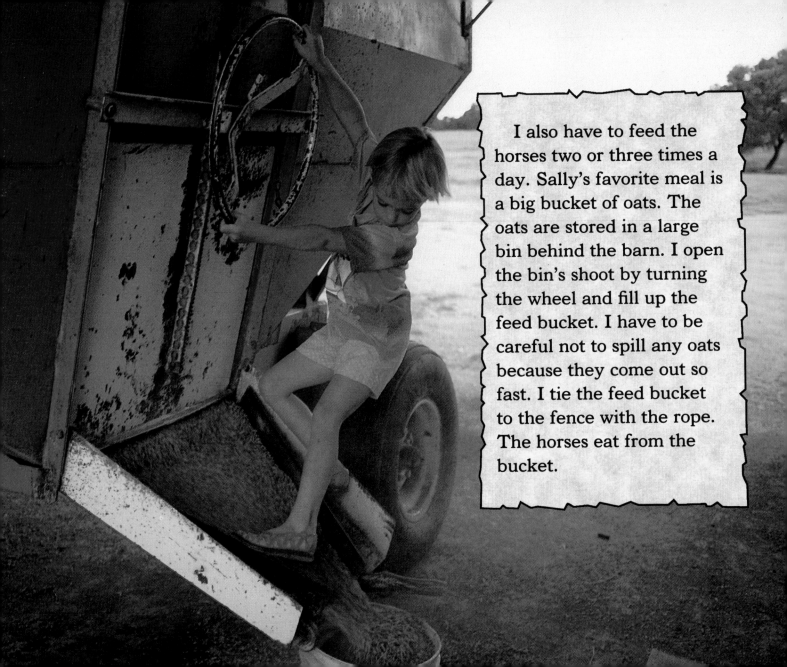

I also have to feed the horses two or three times a day. Sally's favorite meal is a big bucket of oats. The oats are stored in a large bin behind the barn. I open the bin's shoot by turning the wheel and fill up the feed bucket. I have to be careful not to spill any oats because they come out so fast. I tie the feed bucket to the fence with the rope. The horses eat from the bucket.

I'm also in charge of putting maize in the trough for the cows. Vitamins are mixed with the maize to add to their diet of hay and grass.

The cows are shy and won't eat until I've gone.

The ranch animals need a lot of care. Not only do we feed and groom them; we also have Dr. Nottingham, our veterinarian, come to the ranch to give them regular medical checkups. He checks their heartbeats and listens to their lungs to see if they are clear. He also makes sure the horses' hooves are clean. This is very important because any mud or rocks that get stuck in the hooves can cripple the horse. We put new shoes on our horses every eight weeks to help protect their hooves.

Horses are our partners on the ranch. Without them we wouldn't be able to do our jobs. They help us herd the cattle and keep them from running off.

Knowing how to use a lasso is just as important to a cowgirl as knowing how to ride a horse. You have to be able to throw a lasso when you herd cows so you can catch strays.

Even though ranching is hard work, we still find time to have some fun. My family enjoys going to the rodeo whenever we can. A rodeo is a show where cowgirls and cowboys use their ranching skills to compete in different events.

Rodeos are a lot of fun. There are barrel races, bull riding, cattle roping, and even clowns.

Barrel racing is my favorite event. Sally and I often ride in the children's barrel race. In a barrel race you ride your horse around three barrels as fast as you can without knocking them over.

The barrels look like Campbell's soup cans, but there's no soup inside. It's very important to have a horse you can trust and one that trusts you. Barrel racing is easy when you have a horse as smart and fast as Sally.

Before I can ride Sally in a race we both have to get dressed. I like to wear my pink dress boots for big races. Cowgirl boots are very important. They protect your feet and give you support when you ride.

A cowgirl's hat is also very important. When I'm working around the ranch, its wide brim protects me from the heat and the strong sun. But when I'm riding in a race, I move so fast that my father has to put a stampede string on my hat to try to keep it from falling off.

Once I'm dressed, I have to get Sally's gear on. First I cover her with a nice soft blanket to protect her back. Then my dad helps me put her saddle and bridle on. The bridle is the headgear that the reins are attached to. Sally lowers her head to help me dress her.

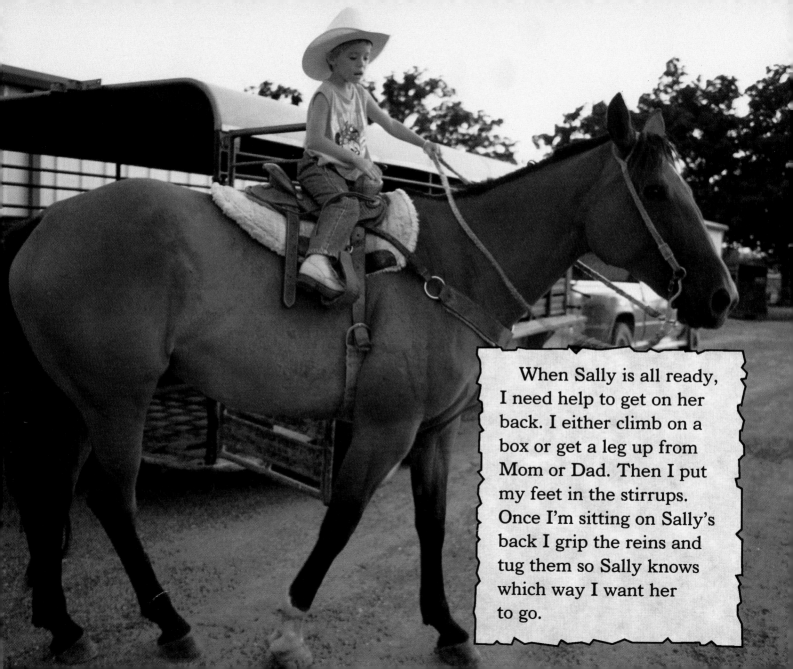

When Sally is all ready, I need help to get on her back. I either climb on a box or get a leg up from Mom or Dad. Then I put my feet in the stirrups. Once I'm sitting on Sally's back I grip the reins and tug them so Sally knows which way I want her to go.

Sally and I are a good team. We've won three
ribbons. But more importantly, we work well together
on the ranch. Someday I hope Sally and I can work on
our own ranch. I already have five cows of my own. I
get one every year for my birthday to get me started. I
hope I will be as good a rancher as my mom.